FOREWORD

Before 1990, there were only eight channels available where a company could communicate with a consumer: at an event, by fax, through direct mail, by telephone, on television, through the radio, on a billboard, or in a print magazine or newsletter. In 2015, there are literally hundreds of channels where consumers access content. Soon, there will be thousands.

Before 1990, large media companies had the most power because they controlled the information channels . . . they controlled the audience. Now 25 years later and that power has almost completely shifted to the consumer. Most consumers have a 24/7 informational device with them at all times where they are free to ignore advertisements and our content about how awesome our product is.

This also means that today anyone, anywhere, can be a publisher and build an audience. We are competing with our traditional competitors for customer attention, as well as our customer's mom's Facebook posts and the blogger down the street. This is a major development in the communications market that impacts every business, large and small.

Because of this sea change, we've seen a major move by companies of all sizes into the practice of content marketing. According to Content Marketing Institute/MarketingProfs research, approximately nine in 10 companies employ some form of content marketing. Wow, that's great. The problem? That same research says that just 30% of organizations are successful at it, and even worse, more than half of those marketers have no idea what success looks like.

Sure, we are fantastic at creating all manner of content – blogs, tweets, posts, podcasts, videos, webinars and more. But we are definitely not good at treating that content as an asset…about building audiences…about consistency over campaigns…about audience focus over product focus…and about quantifying the true value of content.

Content Is Our Differentiator

Don Schultz, the father of integrated marketing and author of Integrated Marketing Communications, discusses the idea that any company, anywhere in the world, can copy everything about what you as a company do . . . except for one thing—how you communicate. The way we communicate with our prospects and customers is the one remaining way we can actually be different.

In their book, Experiences: The 7th Era of Marketing, Robert Rose and Carla Johnson build on Schultz's commentary by adding that it is content, and the experiences that customers have with our content, that is the ultimate differentiator.

But if it's true that content is our true differentiator, and that almost every company on the planet is starting to see the importance of content in marketing, how is it that organizations are actually getting worse at creating and distributing content (the success rate has dropped from 38% to 30%)?

Finding the Why

Here's the answer: content marketing is a new muscle in the organization, and we have no idea how to strengthen it. Marketing professionals are using the marketing and advertising skills of the past, of traditional media, and they don't realize that content is not advertising. We are creating content because we can, and not asking if we should.

That stops today with the book you hold in your hand or are viewing on your device.

Peter Drucker is often quoted as saying, "if you can't measure it, you can't improve it". If we don't articulate and document clear goals for our content, and put structures in place for actually measuring its performance, we will fail. We'd actually be better off not doing anything at all than to keep cluttering up the world with poor, meaningless content.

This book will get you centered. In it, you'll learn the goals behind your content, how those goals become metrics that can be consistently measured, and how those metrics can be quantified into the all elusive R-O-I.

My advice…read this book all the way through. Then, when finished, start back at the beginning and begin to take notes…mark it up…ask questions…create hypotheses…and have some fun with it.

Sure, we are not in 1990 anymore. Cutting through the content clutter is difficult at best. But content marketing gives us the opportunity to truly be different, and perhaps, attain the ultimate outcome…to create better customers.

Good Luck!

Yours in Content,
Joe Pulizzi
Founder, Content Marketing Institute
Author of the best-selling Content Inc. and Epic Content Marketing
Cleveland, Ohio

PREFACE

Why did we write this book?

In May 2011, SAP's then Co-CEO, Bill McDermott, walked onstage at the company's annual SAPPHIRE NOW technology conference. He spoke to the audience about how technology drives competitive advantage for the world's best-run companies. He didn't mention SAP products or services – that would come later. Instead he opened with inspiring stories of innovation from well-known brands that also happened to be SAP customers. In other words, Bill McDermott made SAPs customers the heroes of the stories he told that day.

A few weeks later, McDermott asked his marketing leadership team why these stories of technology-driven innovation and thought leadership were not represented on the SAP company website. Why was SAP product information the only content he could find? Why was this the only way they were communicating to customers and prospects?

Ultimately McDermott challenged his marketing team to change how the brand spoke to its digital audience. That task fell to SAP's then Vice President of Global Marketing and Content Strategy, Michael Brenner. Working with no team and a small budget – but high expectations! -- Michael accepted the challenge to change the way SAP communicated and marketed to customers and prospects – to move from an SAP-centric approach of just talking about the company's products and services, to a customer-centric approach of providing inspiring, informative, and useful content.

Despite the CEO mandate, Michael found that SAP marketers strongly resisted efforts to change their approach. Executives and marketers alike protested saying, "Our job is to sell software. Why would we publish content that doesn't directly sell software?"

But after a year of internal negotiations, partnerships, and compromises, Michael was able to launch SAP's first content marketing site, SAP Business Innovation. The site's business objective was to reach, engage, and ultimately convert early-stage prospects by guiding them through the buyer journey with quality content.

Early into those twelve, challenging months, Michael realized he would only be able to successfully push the initiative through if he conducted intensive research, presented a strong business case, and communicated hard ROI (return on investment) measurement.

And that's exactly what he did. Through this process, Michael identified The Content Formula that eventually helped him gain alignment, support, budget, and proof of the business value of a customer-driven content marketing strategy.

Fast forward to 2015. Michael joined content marketing technology leader NewsCred to help other brands build successful content marketing strategies through consultative workshops and services. In his first year, Michael and his team, Brand Strategy Director Caitlin Domke, and Brand Strategist Liz Bedor, conducted more than two-dozen strategy workshops with brands from various segments and industries.

In those workshops, however, one key challenge emerged more than any other . . .

How Do We Calculate the ROI of Content Marketing?

This is the biggest question we hear from marketers all over the world. Despite the huge surge in the adoption of content marketing, measuring its business impact is complicated. Many marketers still struggle to not only calculate the ROI of their content marketing programs but to also communicate and sell the business value of the tactic internally.

Building on Michael's SAP experience, our work with scores of customers, and hours of comprehensive research, we tackled the challenge of finding specific calculations and approaches to help leading marketers demonstrate the value of content marketing in hard metrics that resonate with business executives of any size, geography, and industry.

But wait, what is content marketing anyway?

Although content marketing isn't new (John Deere began publishing its magazine for farmers in 1895) it is still not widely understood, even by marketing professionals. Some executives are happy to continue promoting their businesses using traditional methods, even though research proves consumers are tuning these out.

Others still view "content" and "content marketing" as the same thing. Worse yet, some see content marketing as "just the latest trend" and believe it will eventually go away. Many senior executives still do not see the business value in consistently providing relevant and helpful content for their customers and prospects.

Content marketing is more than a passing trend. It is not a means to push products and sales pitches. It is much more than "just" content and it is certainly not a passive "native advertisement." **Content marketing is a strategy that actively engages customers to build long-lasting relationships that have real and measurable business value.**

According to the Content Marketing Institute[1], "Content marketing is the marketing and business process for creating and distributing relevant and valuable content to attract, acquire, and engage a clearly defined and understood target audience – with the objective of driving profitable customer action."

At NewsCred, we like to emphasize these aspects when we define content marketing:
• Content marketing is not advertising, or PR, or native ads.
• Content marketing is continuous, always-on, and not campaign-based.
• It is customer-focused, not business-centric.
• Content marketing is owned media. The difference between content marketing and just content is the brand-owned destination where you publish.
• These content marketing properties are financial assets that have real value, and which deliver a return on investment that can be

measured.

This last point is what we intend to cover in this book. The ironic point of the ROI challenge is that for every case in which we have helped a business value their content marketing, the results that come back are not 10, 20, or 30 percent more than the business' overall marketing ROI. The content marketing ROI results are 100, 200, 300 percent more than any traditional marketing tactic.

In these cases, we often see marketing teams struggle with how to approach measuring the effectiveness of their content marketing initiatives. Their real challenge is generally not developing the strategy or content, but rather how to measure their content marketing efforts.

Simply put, these marketers are measuring too narrowly. Vanity metrics such as "likes" and "views" aren't enough on their own merit to analyze the success of an entire marketing program. Content marketers need to be able to calculate the quantifiable value of their content marketing programs. They need numbers they can take to the bank.

In this book, we'll map out how to calculate the impact of content marketing across the business. We'll recommend value-based metrics to benchmark your content marketing initiatives for every business scenario and each business case. As we explain the calculations for calculating ROI, we'll refer to a fictitious company called Software Inc. as an example use case.

Imagine that Software Inc. is a marketing collaboration platform that has been using content marketing for the past two years. The team has done a great job of tracking the costs and performance of their content, but is now struggling to connect the dots in order to communicate and calculate the ROI that content has delivered to the business.

Warning: Math Ahead!

This book will be divided into three main parts, following the process a typical marketer must take to successfully create, execute, and measure a content marketing program. The first explores how to build the business case for content marketing internally. The second dives into how to find the budget for a new content marketing program. Finally, the third covers how to measure content marketing success in business terms.

This is not going to be a riveting story of love, betrayal, and redemption. As much as we wanted to include them, there are no gifs of puppies, kittens, or happy babies in this book :(. However, we realize that marketers, storytellers, editors, writers, and creatives sometimes struggle with tapping into the left side of the brain. Crunching numbers and analyzing data, after all, is hard. It takes work to do the research, build the business case, find the budget, and measure the ROI of anything. We're going to do our best to provide helpful advice, demonstrate practical calculations, and use realistic examples to help bring the key points to life.

We wrote this book because this topic is important. Our goal is to help you develop your own Content Formula, and in the process, become a marketing rock star for your business, your customers, and your career. Thank you for taking the time to read The Content Formula. Enjoy!

~ Michael Brenner and Liz Bedor

PART ONE
/ Build the Business Case

1

The only way to successfully build a business case that will catch the attention of your organization's leadership is to be able to communicate and calculate the ROI of content marketing in real business terms that they can understand.

All marketing programs should be tied to quantifiable results the sales team and executives can easily understand. But what is the ROI of a TV ad, a company's logo on a stadium, or getting press coverage of a product release?

While traditional marketing has always struggled with measuring real business return, digital marketing methods are infinitely more quantifiable.

The way to calculate content marketing ROI varies for each organization. But the initial process for gathering information and building a strong business case can be applied to any business scenario.

You should expect to prepare and present a strong business

case. Otherwise, your content marketing program faces the risks associated with new leadership, budget challenges and the constant pressure on marketing to simply promote the business with more traditional marketing methods.

To help you build a strong business case, here are four steps you can follow.

1. Do Your Research

Before drafting your business case, you need to do your internal research. Find out the costs, ROIs and KPIs of other marketing departments within your organization.

Knowing these numbers upfront will help you to benchmark your program, to get a grasp of what the expectations for success will be, and later, see how you stack up in comparison.

If you are not familiar with the metrics to track down, here are some terms to get you started:

- Average cost per lead
- Customer acquisition cost
- Marketing percentage of customer acquisition cost
- Ratio of customer lifetime value to customer acquisition cost
- Time to payback customer acquisition cost
- Marketing influenced customer percentage
- Marketing originated customer percentage
- Cost per registration (content or events)
- Cost per sale
- Conversion rate
- Average sales for marketing-generated leads
- Marketing-generated pipeline

- Marketing-generated opportunities
- Marketing-generated deals
- Marketing-generated revenue

And if you work for a smaller company, or you just don't have many of the numbers above, try to gather:

- Total marketing budget
- Total marketing ROI
- The total number of leads or sales that your marketing generates overall
- Your budget for each channel (digital, traditional, PR)
- Which programs generate the highest return

Content marketing, like most digital programs, is infinitely more measurable than traditional approaches. So once you understand your overall marketing ROI, you can then begin the process of comparing that to content marketing ROI.

2. Align Program Goals with Company Objectives

The second step to building a business case is to solidify what you will be measuring. Oftentimes content marketers make the mistake of measuring too narrowly, or only focusing on vanity metrics, such as "likes" and "views." While these do indicate engagement, they are not enough on their own merit. Remember, marketers need to be able to measure things that have a quantifiable business impact.

Understanding what metrics other marketing departments are tracking will indicate which key performance indicators (KPI) your organization's leadership cares about most. Does you brand want to boost awareness? Is changing perception and improving brand health most important? Or is the main goal always to drive conversions?

If your company's top priority for the year is to increase conversions, then presenting stellar engagement metrics to leadership will not only leave them unimpressed, but will also show that your program is not aligned with company objectives.

3. Set Appropriate Goals

Once you understand what is expected of your new program and how it will most benefit the company, your third step is to set your program's goals. Knowing the ROI from other marketing departments within your organization (from step 1) will help you with this.

This knowledge will allow you to set goals that are realistic and necessary in order for your content marketing program to be considered a success. If you proudly present that your program has driven 100 conversions, while other marketing departments drive 1,000, leadership will consider your program as an ineffective use of time and resources.

Setting these expectations upfront will enable you to manage your program efficiently. If halfway through the year, your engagement metrics are consistently strong but unique reach is dwindling, you'll be able to reinvest into distribution before it's too late to meet your goals.

This is a great time to mention that content marketing typically does not produce results in a short period of time. Content marketing requires continuous investment, testing and optimization. It often takes 6-12 months to demonstrate business value. We call this the "content marketing learning curve." When setting your goals, make sure to give yourself enough time to reach the finish line.

4. Ask for a Realistic Budget

The final step to building your business case is to request a fair and reasonable budget. Marketing budgets can vary from thousands to millions of dollars, depending on your organization. Having an idea of the amount allotted to fund other marketing departments will help you decide how ambitious or humble your content marketing program should be.

If you're unsure of what type of budget you can ask for, present the options of a pilot program and six to twelve months to test and learn. It's important to adjust your program goals along with your budget size, as is it simply unrealistic to drive "champagne results on a beer budget."

Depending on your organization, your best strategy can be to ask for the moon and the stars, with the hope of just getting the moon.

Oftentimes, content marketing doesn't *require additional investment.* In this book, we will help you identify ways to fund content marketing programs from an existing underperforming marketing budget.

EXAMPLE: HOW MICHAEL BUILT THE BUSINESS CASE AT SAP

Despite having the mandate of the CEO and support from marketing leadership, Michael found resistance to the idea of creating helpful, non-promotional content for the SAP website.

To build the business case for this, he turned to web search data. Michael found that there was a significantly larger digital audience using early-stage, unbranded search terms such as "big data" over late-stage, SAP product terms such as "HANA." Essentially this means there are many more early-stage prospects just starting their buyer journey than late-stage prospects who are likely ready to purchase.

Michael then looked at how many of those early-stage, unbranded searches were finding their way to the SAP website. The answer? Almost none. Most of the website's traffic was from branded, late-stage product searches. (This was before Google masked most inbound search keywords.)

So what did this mean? SAP did not show up when prospects asked search engines early-stage questions such as, "What is big data?" Because of all the promotional, branded content on SAP's website, search engines determined that it was not the best place for these early-stage prospects to find answers to their questions.

Consequently, early-stage potential customers who were looking for answers to questions were not directed to the SAP website. The people who were finding their way to the SAP website were very late-stage buyers who likely had already decided to purchase an SAP product since they were searching for those branded terms. Essentially, the website's content was ignoring the audience they most wanted to talk to.

Sales executives understand the power of showing up first in Google. With the low amount of early-stage search traffic and the poor search ranking results for important unbranded solution keywords, Michael was able to build the business case to move ahead with his content marketing program.

<u>NOTES</u>

PART TWO
/ Find the Budget

2

Sometimes it can be difficult for companies to carve out sufficient budget to fund new content marketing programs. While overcoming this obstacle is often a tricky proposition, we can find this budget if we look in the right places.

Calculate the Costs of Unused Content

Before deciding on your budget, we need to have a solid understanding of your organization's current content costs and utilization. Every organization creates content, so let's start with calculating those costs.

The first step is to conduct an audit for a sample of the volume of content your organization produces. Take one product line, one persona, or one market unit and make sure to capture all the content that smaller team creates. Make sure to include agency work, campaigns, web copy, and even sales enablement materials.

Or if this seems like too big a task, take an even smaller slice of data from a random sample of the content from one area of your business.

Next apply an average cost in order to gain a sense for the size of the problem. When calculating this, keep in mind to include the costs of freelancers, salaries, technologies, et cetera.

Before Software Inc. decided to invest in content marketing, the team performed a content audit to understand how much the company was wasting on unused content. On average, Software Inc. had been creating 1,200 pieces of content per year with an average cost of $200 each. **Therefore, Software Inc. has spent $240,000 on content each year.**

Next, we need to understand how much of your organization's content actually gets used. **On average, 60–70% of content goes completely unused.**[2]

Content that gets created but never used is 100% waste! It never gets the chance to reach an audience.

Based on this information, we can take Software Inc.'s production costs and subtract the amount that was being used to find how much money the company was wasting on unused content.

COST OF UNUSED CONTENT

Current Production Costs
- Amount that gets used
_____

= How much money is wasted on unused content

So for this example, **Software Inc. was wasting between $144,000 and $168,000 on unused content every year.** From these calculations, the team realized a planned and documented content marketing strategy would provide a platform to share the unused content, reuse and repurpose it in different ways, extending its shelf life and putting it to use.

Once you identify content production that never gets used, it's important to understand why this content was created in the first place. Unused content is often created for the following reasons:

- Because it's what you've always done
- Because an executive asked for it
- Campaigns that lose funding half-way through the program
- Managers leave and their programs get canceled

Whatever the reasons, gain the commitment from your management team to stop creating content that never gets used. And reallocate the budget to creating content that your customers want.

At SAP, Michael found that a large majority of the content produced in one product line went completely unused. So he started to track down the causes of this content waste across the company and was able to find ways to re-purpose that content for no additional investment.

Borrow Budget from Underperforming Digital Assets

The next place we can look for budget is from the opportunity costs of underperforming digital assets, such as advertising.

As consumers, we are all tuning out advertising. Consider:

• The average click-through rate of display ads is 0.1%[3].
• Only 8% of Internet users account for 85% of clicks on display ads (and some aren't even humans!)[4].
• About half (50%) of clicks on mobile ads are accidental[5].
• Nearly 10% of the Internet users in the US use ad-blocking software and that number is growing rapidly[6].

The solution is to recycle inefficient or unused resources to fund a fresh content marketing program. Asking for a small percentage of a larger advertising budget is an excellent place to start looking for budget donations.

Approach Budgeted Teams with a Partnership Opportunity

Another way to find budget for content marketing is through a partnership with other departments that already have budget.

EXAMPLE: HOW SAP ADVERTISING BUDGETS PAID FOR THEIR CONTENT MARKETING

As we mentioned, while at SAP, Michael was tasked with building a content marketing platform to showcase SAP thought leadership in the area of technology and innovation. However, he had little support from the more traditional marketing teams. And he had no budget!

In conversations with the head of advertising, he learned that they spent a good amount of money every year on campaign landing pages for advertising. When he looked at the data behind those pages from previous campaigns, he saw more than a 95% bounce rate, zero organic search traffic, and no social shares. How could something so expensive drive so little engagement?

So he proposed to the team that they give him **half their landing page budget to build their landing pages.** He agreed to allow them to define the branding, whatever copy they wanted and also to include the right calls-to-action.

But instead of building a one-time-use landing page, he built a dynamic content marketing platform. Advertising traffic was simply landing on one of the pages of this new site. The rest of the traffic would come from articles his team would publish every day on the topics relevant to their audience.

So when they said yes, he was able to fund the creation of a content marketing platform that also served as the landing page for advertising. The traffic from ad campaigns was supplemented by organic search traffic, social shares, a lower bounce rate and higher engagement with the brand.

Michael saved the advertising team half their landing page budget and used the other half to build the content marketing platform the company needed to reach early-stage buyers, while also driving awareness and higher brand engagement in support of the company's advertising efforts.

That money he saved delivered a 100% ROI before he even published one article!

Approaching other teams that already have budget with the opportunity for a partnership is a great way to put your content marketing strategy to action, while also building internal champions within your organization.

In Michael's case, once he was able to deliver the platform, his program proved its value and was able to justify funding in its own right.

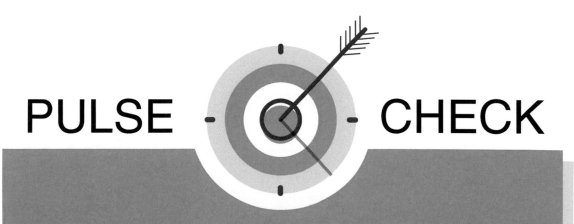

PULSE - CHECK

FINDING A BUDGET

find the budget for your online marketing campaign, **calculate the costs of unused content, borrow budget from underperforming digital assets, and approach budgeted teams with partnership opportunities.**

The solution: A planned content marketing strategy that provides a platform to share unused content, reuse, and repurpose it in different ways, thereby extending its shelf-life and putting it to use.

<u>NOTES</u>

PART THREE
/ Measure the Business Case

3

The promise of content marketing is to earn your audience with value versus buying it with advertising. With traditional paid advertising methods, you are buying reach at some frequency, but the audience is likely not very engaged.

In short, traditional ads are about as effective as screaming into the wind. Content marketing, on the other hand, starts with the goals of earning your target audience's attention by providing a differentiated value based on their needs and interests.

That is why measuring content marketing is so important. Now that you have built and funded your business case, we need to measure the success of your content marketing program in one of four ways: brand awareness, brand health, conversions and retention.

Brand Awareness

Increasing brand awareness, or the extent to which consumers are familiar with your brand, is one of the most common content marketing business cases.

When asked about the success of your brand awareness, consider how relevant you are to the conversation. In other words, how many of your early-stage prospects (your target consumers) are finding their way to your company website?

We can measure brand awareness in three different ways:

• Paid vs. organic search traffic
• Unbranded organic search traffic
• Organic search share of voice

How to Calculate the Value of Paid vs. Organic Search Traffic

Paid search traffic is the search traffic your site receives from paid search advertisements. Organic search traffic is the search traffic your site receives due to a high organic search ranking. Not only is organic search traffic free, but it also indicates that your company is relevant to a wide customer base.

To calculate the value of this, we want to compare how much we're paying for traffic versus earning organically. This can easily be calculated via Google Analytics. First, go to "Acquisition." Next, go to "Campaigns" and then "Organic Keywords."

In October 2011, Google changed the way it harvests data for user privacy reasons. Because of this, Google can still see the keywords used to perform searches, but Google Analytics account owners cannot. While this keyword information would be helpful, we can still see the number and percentage of sessions from organic keyword search, which is all we need to calculate its value.

Based on Software Inc.'s Google Analytics, the company's site received 750,000 visits from organic search traffic, totaling roughly 75% of sessions over the past year.

Next, we want to see how much paid traffic we're receiving, which we can also find in Google Analytics. Again, go to "Acquisition" and then "campaigns," Then, instead of "Organic Keywords, select "Paid Keywords."

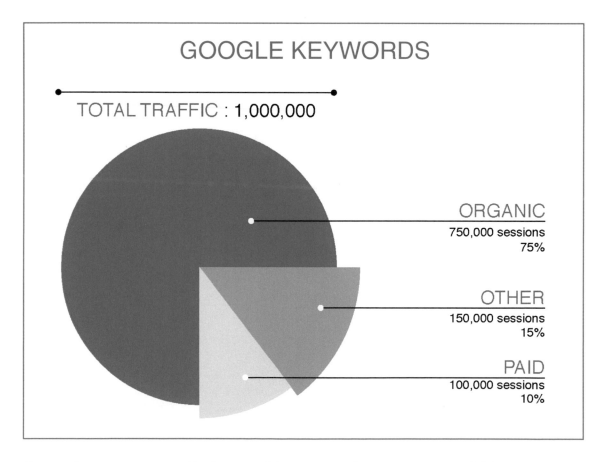

Over the past year, Software Inc. spent $50,000 on paid keywords, driving about 100,000 visits in paid search traffic. Based on these numbers and percentages, we can calculate the value of Software Inc.'s organic traffic.

ORGANIC
SEARCH TRAFFIC

($50,000 X 750,000) / 100,000 = $375,000

Simply multiply the money spent ($50,000) with the organic search traffic (750,000). Then, divide that number by the paid search traffic (100,000). **The resulting amount of $375,000 is how much the organic search traffic is worth.**

If your company is spending money on paid search ads, just ask them what their average cost per click is. If they are spending $2 per click and you can earn 100,000 visitors organically for the same search terms, then the value of that traffic is $200,000.

One of the biggest promises of content marketing is to rank organically for search terms you are currently buying. This value is easy to measure and the cost savings are evident to any business executive.

How to Calculate the Value of Unbranded Organic Search Traffic

Unbranded organic search traffic is search traffic your site receives from keywords that never mention your brand name or products.

Any visitor who searches your brand name already knows where they want to go. Unbranded organic traffic is important to calculate because we want to know about the people who didn't know where they would end up.

They had a question or a need, asked a search engine for direction, and that interaction brought them to you. Market Research Company, IDC, said it best with, "The buyer journey is nothing more than a series of questions that must be answered[7]."

To calculate unbranded organic search, we need to exclude your brand or products' name from the search. To do this, create an "Advanced Filter" on your Google Analytics that will exclude those branded keywords. For Software Inc., the brand and products contain the word, "Software."

Organic
Unbranded Traffic

($50,000 X 500,000) / 100,000 = $250,000

For this example, let's say the results showed that now with excluding branded keywords, **Software Inc.'s unbranded organic search traffic accounts for 500,000 visits, or about 50% of total traffic.** As we did earlier, multiply the money spent ($50,000) with the unbranded organic search traffic (500,000). Then, divide that number by the paid search traffic (100,000) to learn the worth of organic unbranded traffic ($250,000).

Based on those calculations, we find that organic unbranded search traffic is worth $250,000.

At SAP, Michael found that 99.9% of the traffic coming to SAP websites was branded search. These visitors were already aware of SAP and what it sold. On the contrary, the size of the audience asking unbranded search questions like "What is CRM software?" was in some cases 3,000 times larger than the audience searching for branded terms like "SAP CRM."

The company's website, however, wasn't reaching any of those early-stage prospects because almost all the content SAP had on its site was promotional and branded. This gap represented a huge opportunity to reach, engage and convert early-stage buyers the company currently was ignoring.

The results of this analysis led Michael's team to focus on those unbranded keywords with the highest volume and lowest competition. This ensured that their content marketing efforts would reach the right people and give them the highest chance for success in measuring conversions.

Using the average cost per click for paid search ads, Michael was able to calculate the value of the traffic he earned organically. This ultimately led to more content creation and distribution funding for his program.

How to Calculate the Value of Organic Search Share of Voice

Organic search share of voice is the percentage of online conversations in your space that include your brand. Essentially, it measures how much your brand or product is talked about compared to your competitors.

To calculate the value of this, we first want to choose a group of words based around your brand's product or service. When choosing your keywords, be sure to stay within a common theme. In general, it's better for your search engine optimization (SEO) strategy to focus heavily on a specific topic, rather than lightly on many topics.

For Software Inc. we want to keep our keywords focused: *marketing collaboration, marketing automation, marketing software, marketing lead management, email marketing.*

Next, choose your competition. Who do you want to compare your brand against? When doing this, be sure to know your competitors' URLs. Some may use off-branded URLs for their content marketing efforts.

Once you have yours and your competitors' URLs, search your selected keywords in Google and record the organic search rankings for each keyword you selected for yourself and your competitors. For example, if your site is the top result when you search for your product category in Google, your ranking is #1.

If you do rank, record in what position. (Note: You can rank more than once.) When doing this, keep in mind there's no point in looking at more than the top 10, because only 2% of users travel to the 2nd page of Google. Your chart should look something like Graphic B.

GRAPHIC B

MARKETING COLLABORATION
RANKING #1

10	9	8	7	6	5	4	3	2	1

1st position

RANKING #2

10	9	8	7	6	5	4	3	2	

2nd position

RANKING #3

10	9	8	7	6	5	4	3		

3rd position

MARKETING AUTOMATION
RANKING #1

10	9	8	7	6	5	4	3	2	

2nd position

RANKING #2

10	9	8	7	6	5	4	3		

3rd position

RANKING #3

10	9	8	7	6	5	4			

4th position

MARKETING SOFTWARE
RANKING #1

10	9	8	7	6	5	4	3	2	

2nd position

RANKING #2

MARKETING LEAD MANAGEMENT
RANKING #1

10	9	8	7	6	5				

5th position

RANKING #2

EMAIL MARKETING
RANKING #1

Now that you have your rankings documented we want to calculate your share of voice via average click through rates for each position. To do this, we can use the 2014 Google Click Through Rates chart below in Graphic C.

Every year Google publishes[8] its click through rates for each position, so be sure to use the most recent rates you can find. For our purposes, we'll use Google's Click Through Rates from 2014.

GRAPHIC C

GOOGLE CLICK THROUGH RATES										
POSITION	1	2	3	4	5	6	7	8	9	10
CLICK THROUGH RATE	31.24	14.04	9.85	6.97	5.5	3.73	0	0	0	0

If you rank for a keyword more than once, simply add the click through rates to find the keyword's total share of voice. So in our example, the word "marketing collaboration" has a share of voice of 55.13% after adding the three rankings together.

SHARE OF VOICE

31.24 + 14.04 + 9.85 = 55.13%

**TOTAL
SHARE OF VOICE**

(55.13 + 30.86 + 14.04 + 5.5 + 0) / 5 = 26,38%

To find your overall share of voice, average the share of voice for all of your keywords. For this example, we add the total share of voice for each keyword (55.13 + 30.86 + 14.04 + 5.5 + 0) and divide by our total number of keywords (5). Based on these calculations, we can determine that our **total share of voice is 26.38%**. For further clarity, consult Graphic D.

GRAPHIC D

KEYWORD	RANKING #1	RANKING #2	RANKING #3	SHARE OF VOICE
MARKETING COLLABORATION	31.24	14.04	9.85	55.13%
MARKETING AUTOMATION	14.04	9.85	6.97	30.86%
MARKETING SOFTWARE	14.04			14.04%
MARKETING LEAD MANAGEMENT	5.5			5.5%
EMAIL MARKETING				
TOTAL SHARE OF VOICE				26,38%

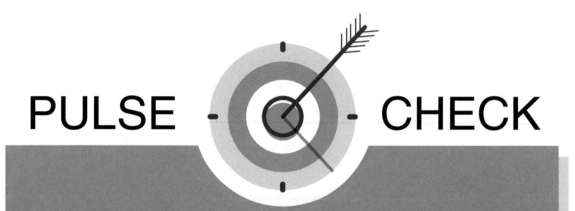

PULSE - ⊙ - CHECK

MEASURING BRAND AWARENESS

Brand awareness measures how many of your early-stage prospects find your company website.

Brand awareness can be measured by calculating the value of **paid versus organic search traffic, unbranded organic search traffic,** and **organic search share of voice.**

Organic search traffic is the search traffic your site receives due to a high organic search ranking. Organic search traffic is free and indicates that your company is relevant to a wide customer base.

Unbranded organic search traffic is search traffic your site receives from keywords that never mention your brand name or products. A high amount of unbranded organic search traffic indicates that you answer a customer s question or need.

Organic search share of voice measures how much your brand or product is talked about compared to your competitors.

As a rule of thumb, your share of voice should be close to your market share. If you have x% of the sales in a product category, you have the potential to achieve that same % share of voice.

In our fictitious example, Software Inc. has about 25% of the market share, so 26% share of voice is just about right for them. You can represent this as a "fair share of voice index," so 20 (26% / 25%) *100 = a fair share of voice index of 104.

If you notice a gap between your market share and your share of voice, however, that means your competition is wooing your prospects before you!

If you don't want to go through the manual trouble, there are a few tools that will help you calculate this. The first, Quick Sprout[9,] allows you to enter up to 3 competitor sites and get a ranking on scores for each. The second, SEMrush[10], offers a free search analysis for your site and your competitors.

Brand Health

Content marketing can be described as the art of communicating with your customers and prospects without stelling. If your brand is like most, however, your content marketing probably promotes the brand too much…and your audience learns to tune you out.

David Beebe, Vice President of Global Creative and Content Marketing for Marriott International explains, **"Content marketing is like a first date. If all you do is talk about yourself, there won't be a second date."** You have to let people get to know your brand, like your brand, and then eventually trust your brand enough to buy from you.

Brand Health is a great business case for content marketing once you've already achieved sufficient brand awareness. You've accomplished the goal of letting people get to know your brand, but do you know how much they like your brand?

Social sentiment is one of the ways some companies have tried to measure brand health in social media interactions. Many businesses, however, quickly see that social sentiment is hard to track effectively, it only measures those who mention your brand on social, and it often changes very little.

Content marketing brand health metrics allow you to measure how your entire digital audience feels about you based on real actions they take (or don't take) with your content.

If you want to create a relationship with your customers, brand health is how you measure that relationship in two different but equally important perspectives: engagement and audience growth.

There are five ways to measure engagement.

• Time on site
• Repeat visitors
• Social likes
• Subscriptions
• Bounce rates

There are three ways to measure audience growth.

• Paid versus organic search traffic
• Social shares/Followers
• Share of voice/Offsite SEO

Let's focus first on how to measure engagement.

How to Calculate the Value of Time on Site

"Time on site" means exactly what you think: how much time are visitors spending on your website? At first, we naturally assume we should aim for high time on site, right? Not necessarily. Not all time on site is equal. When determining your brand's time on site goals, it's important to keep in mind why someone is going to your site.

There are four categories your business can uniquely fall into:

• High time on site, low number of page views
• High time on site, high number of page views
• Low time on site, low number of page views
• Low time on site, high number of page views

First, your business can experience **a high time on site, but a low number of page views.** This may indicate a reading behavior pattern. This can be good for sites that require a lot of time to read and understand the contents of the site, such as a professional services company.

Second, your business can experience **a high time on site and a high number of page views.** In general, content marketing hubs and company blogs should aim for this type of engagement, as it may indicate a high level of interest and involvement with your site. At the same time, a high number of page views and time on site could also indicate users having difficulty navigating your site to find what they're looking for. In that scenario, this type of engagement would be poor for transactional websites, such as banking.

Third, your business can experience **a low time on site and low number of page views.** This can indicate that the site only provides a simple response or quick answer, and is a good indicator for sites where visitors are seeking quick answers, such as directories. In this case, repeat visitor behavior is a crucial contributing factor.

Unfortunately, the low time on site and low number of page views generally implies customer disinterest in the site, which is a poor indicator for most content marketing sites.

Last, your business can experience **a low time on site, but a high number of page views.** This may indicate success for sites that require visitors to complete tasks quickly. However, this could also indicate that visitors are lost in the site, become frustrated and leave. Content marketers want to avoid this time on site engagement.

In general, content marketing programs should aim for high time on site and high number of page views.

Measuring time on site is also a great way to optimize the effectiveness of your content marketing programs. Compare the time on site for different types of content like articles, videos, list posts, long form posts. You can also measure the time on site for traffic from different paid content distribution providers such as Outbrain versus LinkedIn versus Facebook.

How to Calculate the Value of Repeat Visitors

Calculating repeat visitors measures the number of times someone engages with your brand. New visitors are important, but repeat visitors are great for two reasons: they're less expensive and are more likely to buy from you.

First, repeat visitors are less expensive, because once you "have" a new reader **you don't have to spend time and money attracting that reader.** Your content is sufficient to have them coming back.

Second, if the ultimate goal of your content marketing is to sell a product or service, you're much more likely to sell to visitors who come back time after time. **96% of people visiting your site aren't actually ready to purchase**[11], so brands need to think of other ways to bring prospects back.

If brands can do this successfully, those same prospects will ultimately choose them when they're ready to purchase.
Now that we understand why repeat visitors are important, let's dive into how to measure their value.

Repeat Visitor Ratio (RVR) measures the percentage of visitors who return to your site after an initial visit. **The higher your RVR is, the better your site is at engaging the average new visitor.**

To put a monetary value on RVR, we first need to calculate your current RVR. So far this month, Software Inc. has received 4,000 visitors and 800 were repeat visitors.

REPEAT
VISITOR RATIO

800 / 4,000 = 20%

Divide the total visitors (4,000) by the repeat visitors (800) to get the RVR. Thus, Software Inc.'s **RVR is 20%.**

To put a monetary value on RVR, we need to look at the average amount you're spending in advertising to drive net new traffic to your site. For our example, Software Inc. is spending $5,000 per month on advertising to drive new visitors. If 80%, or 3,200 visitors are net new, they're spending an average of $1.56 per visitor.

We can reach this value by dividing the number of visitors by the amount you're spending to get this number.

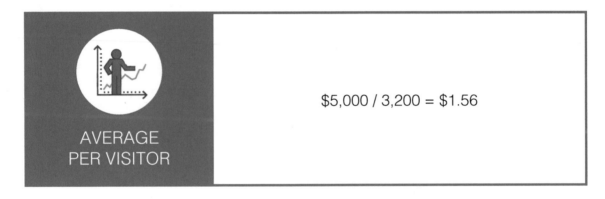

AVERAGE
PER VISITOR

$5,000 / 3,200 = $1.56

Taking that finding, we can then calculate the value of Software Inc.'s 800 repeat visitors. Simply multiply the average amount you're spending per visitor ($1.56) by the repeat visitors (800).

VALUE
OF SOFTWARE

800 X $1.56 = $1,250

Therefore, Software Inc.'s repeat visitors are valued at $1,250 per month.

There are four ways to improve your RVR. The first step is to **better target your market** to ensure you're spending to reach the right audience.

The second step is to **provide great content consistently.** All the advertising in the world won't improve engagement if your audience doesn't find your content interesting, entertaining, or valuable.

Third, **ensure site navigation is streamlined and intuitive.** If visitors can't identify with your website, they likely won't identify with your content. Lure them in with a unique, seamless experience.

Finally, **constantly create new content to keep the site fresh and relevant.** Relevancy has a deadline and visitors know they have millions of other sites at their disposal. Make sure you're always leading the conversation to keep visitors coming back.

As you work on increasing the percentage of repeat visitors, **don't forget to also increase the total number of visitors.** Otherwise, you'll start preaching to the same choir. We suggest testing different approaches to achieve the right balance.

How to Calculate the Value of Social Likes

Social likes measure which content is resonating most with your audience. These "likes" serve as a **light indicator** for whether or not your target audience is responding to your promoted content.

While many have tried, it's difficult to assess real value in a "like." However, it's important to **track social shares** over time to ensure your content is reaching a baseline or increasing level of engagement.

How to Calculate the Value of Subscriptions

Subscription is the hottest metric of content marketing success today because new subscribers measure reach, engagement and conversion all in one metric.

Subscribers are people giving your brand exclusive access to their inbox, opening the opportunity for you to market to them. Because of this, your email list is an asset, and should be valued as such.

At SAP, Michael found that subscribers were 10 times more likely to convert to a lead, an event registration, and ultimately, sales revenue.

The first step to calculating the value of your subscribers is to find your maximum allowable cost threshold for getting a new subscriber. If you don't know this, you could be spending more to obtain subscribers than those subscribers are actually worth. Knowing your cost to obtain a new subscriber is the only way to determine how much **you can actually afford** to invest in growing your list sign-up and what your maximum allowable cost to obtain a new subscriber should be.

As a rule of thumb, **your subscriber cost per acquisition (CPA) should be well under your average sale amount from a new customer and within range of what you pay to obtain other valuable actions,** such as webinar sign-ups, free content downloads, or even direct sales.

First, let's calculate what it actually costs for Software Inc. to get a new subscriber from each list-building method. For this example, please reference Graphic E.

Now we need to determine Software Inc.'s maximum allowable

GRAPHIC E

METHOD	QUANTITY OF SUBSCRIBERS (QOS)	COST PER ACQUISITION (QPA)
FACEBOOK	200	$2.30
TWITTER	400	$1.00
PAID SEARCH	300	$2.00
WEBINAR	100	$0.10

CPA for acquiring a new list member, and continue to invest in the methods that fall at or below your CPA. Let's say the team tested a few tactics and decided that their maximum allowable CPA for a new email address is $1.50. Moving forward, they'll want to continue pursuing all methods costing $1.50 or less. So instead of focusing on Facebook (CPA of $2.30) or paid search (CPA of $2.00), they should focus their efforts on Twitter (CPA of $1.00) and webinar (CPA of $0.10).

Over time, Software Inc. needs to also measure the **quality of the subscribers on your list** by monitoring things like average sale value and unsubscribe rate. When we analyze the data, we're easily able to spot the methods that produce the best quality and quantity of subscribers within the allowable CPA. The higher the quality of subscribers you attract, the **more likely they are to convert** to becoming not only customers, but also your best customers – resulting in more revenue from which to raise your CPA.

To calculate the value per subscriber for Software Inc., we need to find the difference between the sale value and cost per acquisition for the subscribers.

To do this, we use the formula below:

VALUE PER SUBSCRIBER

(QOS X ASV X (1 – UR) – QOS X CPA) / QOS

= VALUE PER SUBSCRIBER

METHOD	QUANTITY OF SUBSCRIBERS (QOS)	COST PER ACQUISITION (QPA)	UNSUBSCRIBE RATE (UR)	AVERAGE SALE VALUE (ASV)
FACEBOOK	200	$2.30	30%	$100
TWITTER	400	$1.00	5%	$100
PAID SEARCH	300	$2.00	15%	$150
WEBINAR	100	$0.10	5%	$200

Let's use Facebook Ads as an example.

VALUE PER
SUBSCRIBER

(200 X 100 * (1 – 0.30) – 200 X 2.30) / 200

= VALUE PER SUBSCRIBER

First we'll subtract the unsubscribe rate (0.30) from 1. Then we'll multiply that number (0.70) by the quantity of subscribers (200) and the average sale value ($100). This will equal 14,000. Next, multiply the cost per acquisition ($2.30) by the quantity of subscribers. This will equal 460. Subtract 460 from 14,000 and divide that number by the quantity of subscribers **Therefore, the value of each Facebook subscription is $67.70.**

We used the same formula to find the value per subscriber for the other three methods, as seen in Graphic F.

GRAPHIC F

METHOD	QUANTITY OF SUBSCRIBERS (QOS)	COST PER ACQUISITION (CPA)	UNSUBSCRIBE RATE (UR)	AVERAGE SALE VALUE (ASV)	TOTAL VALUE (TV)	VALUE PER SUBSCRIBER (VPS)
FACEBOOK	200	$2.30	30%	$100	$13,540	$67.70
TWITTER	400	$1.00	5%	$100	$37,600	$94
PAID SEARCH	300	$2.00	15%	$150	$37,650	$125.50
WEBINAR	100	$0.10	5%	$200	$18,990	$189.90

Based on these calculations, we can see that **paid search and webinar methods return the most value per subscriber.**

However, since paid search's CPA is more expensive than the maximum allowance of $1.50, **Software Inc. should defer to webinar and Twitter tactics.**

How to Calculate the Value of Bounce Rate

The bounce rate is a metric which indicates the percentage of visitors who land on one of your web pages and then leave, rather than continuing to view other pages.

A high bounce rate is a reason for concern since it indicates that your **website visitors aren't looking for more content on your site, clicking on calls-to-action, or converting into subscribers.**

Since attracting and converting visitors into qualified leads is the main objective for content marketing, this is an important metric to measure and improve.

The most common question we hear about bounce rate is, "How should my site stack up?" Ultimately it really depends on your industry and site type, but in general, here are some accepted industry benchmarks[12]:

- Campaign landing pages have high bounce rates due to high promotional content: 70% — 90%
- Retail sites drive well-targeted traffic that is "ready-to-buy:" 20% — 40%
- Content websites are somewhere in the middle: 40% — 60%

Visitors bounce for two reasons. Once, they didn't find what they were looking for, and two, the page didn't provide the kind of experience the visitor was looking for. The natural question is then, **"what can I do to improve my site's bounce rate?"**

There are generally five approaches to lowering bounce rates:

1. **Attract the right people.** You want visitors to your site to come because you are answering an important question or search query. So make sure your headlines are clear, your topics are well defined and the content delivers on the promise made in the headline.
2. **Great design.** Use colors, large fonts, images, white space and a great mobile experience to make reading your content easy.
3. **Mobile-friendly.** Mobile visitors generally have higher bounce rates due to the responsiveness of the website. Your site should be designed so mobile visitors can easily scan and read your content.
4. **Load time.** Slow load times are a big factor in search engine rankings because the slower the site is to load, the more people bounce. Make every effort to decrease page load times by optimizing photos, set external links to open in a new window, and remove unwanted ads and popups from your site experience.
5. **Publish great content.** Nothing will keep visitors on your site from bouncing more than high-quality content. Quality includes more than just great writing. Make sure to also include proper grammar and spelling, as well as the use of quality design, navigation, text size, fonts and images to support the text.

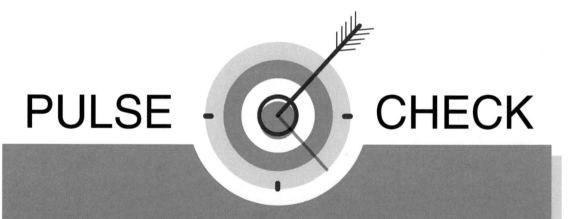

PULSE - CHECK

MEASURING ENGAGEMENT

Engagement is more a measure of your content performance and is often a means to the end goal of conversions.

Subscribers provide the opportunity to measure reach, engagement and conversion all in one metric and should be the focus of any content marketing program.

While engagement is difficult to place a real business value on, increases in engagement are a sign that your content is attracting the right audience. And subscribers have real business value that can be calculated in hard dollars.

Now, let's focus on the second way to measure brand health — audience growth. Remember, there are three ways to measure audience growth: paid versus organic search traffic, social shares/followers, and share of voice/offsite SEO.

How to Calculate the Value of Paid vs. Organic Search Traffic

Remember, paid search traffic is the search traffic your site receives from paid search advertisements whereas organic search traffic is the search traffic your site receives due to a high organic search ranking.

With organic search, you can literally earn your audience's attention instead of buying it.

To calculate the value of this, we want to compare how much you're paying for traffic versus earning organically. These calculations are the same for when measuring the brand awareness that we talked about earlier.

How to Calculate the Value of Social Shares/Followers

The term "followers" refers to users who have subscribed to updates on your brand's social accounts. "Shares" refers to people who shared your content because they felt it was interesting and would resonate with their social network.

While social shares can be seen as an engagement metric, they should also be quantified as a free source of distribution and reach. Let's say Software Inc. spends about $1,000 on paid social distribution and reached 5,000 viewers. **For this example, each view was worth $0.20.** We can reach this value by dividing the number of views (5,000) by the amount spent on social distribution ($1,000).

Now let's say a social post was shared organically by Software Inc.'s followers and reached 500 viewers. Based on the value of each view from our paid distribution, we can also value the 500 organic views at $0.20 each, or $100 total.

Brands should also track if their social follower growth positively correlates with their total number of shares. If it does, this would indicate that your organic social shares are reaching the right audience for your brand.

How to Calculate the Value of Share of Voice/ Offsite SEO

Share of voice and offsite SEO simply measures what third parties say about you. Google has stated it considers over 200 factors in its search ranking algorithm, with some variables weighted with more importance than others.

While no one knows the exact algorithm, there is one thing virtually all SEO experts agree upon: **The number and quality of links coming into your site, or offsite SEO**, is near the top of the list. When you think about it, heavily weighting this importance makes sense. You can say great things about yourself on your site, but it means considerably more for an objective and reputable third party to reference you as an expert.

The way to measure your offsite SEO is to look at your inbound links and their value. An easy way to do this is by plugging your site's URL into Moz's Fresh Web Explorer[13], which allows you to see all inbound links, see your top-linked pages, sort by linking domains, and see the anchor text other sites use to link you. **You should also do the same with your competitor's sites and compare the results to see how you stand.**

When analyzing the results, there are a few things to keep in mind.

First, scan your site's highest-authority inbound links and think of opportunities to get other similar links. Scan your competitors' highest-authority inbound links and ask, "Do they provide any ideas for obtaining similar links?" Can you get those links too?
Be aware that inbound links from non-profit (.org) and education (.edu) sites are especially powerful. Above all, remember to build your inbound links gradually. Google algorithms will notice a quick accumulation of links and may penalize as a result.

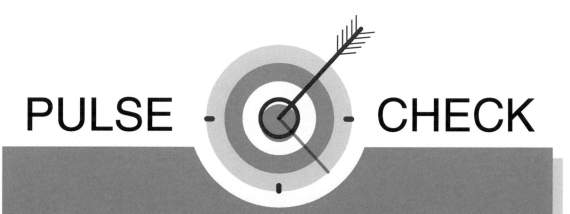

PULSE - - CHECK

MEASURING BRAND HEALTH

Brand health measures how your digital audience feels about you. Brand health can be measured through **engagement** and **audience growth.**

There are five ways to measure engagement:
- **Time on site -** the amount of time visitors spend on your site
- **Repeat visitors -** the number of times someone engages with your brand
- **Social likes -** which content is resonating most with your audience
- **Subscriptions -** marketing directly to people s inboxes
- **Bounce rates -** the percentage of visitors who leave your site without viewing other pages

To improve your Repeat Visitor Ration (RVR), better target your marketing, provide great content, ensure site navigation is streamlined and intuitive, and constantly create new content to keep the site fresh and relevant.

To improve your site s bounce rate, **attract the right visitors, enhance usability, use a good layout, speed up page load,** and **provide good content.**

There are three ways to measure audience growth: **paid versus organic search traffic, social shares/ followers,** and **share of voice/ offsite SEO.**
- **Paid versus organic search traffic**—search traffic your site receives from paid search advertisements vs. traffic due to a high organic search ranking
- **Social shares/ followers**—users who have subscribed to updates on your brand s social accounts
- **Share of voice/ offsite SEO**—what "they" say about you

Conversions

The third way to determine the success of your content marketing program is to measure conversions. **This may be the most valued business case for content marketing.** Many marketing leaders and business executives, however, want to jump too quickly into projecting conversions before you've published your first post.

The fact is that content marketing conversions *only come after you've reached and consistently engaged the right audience with content that helps them.*

Chances are your first approach to driving conversions won't work. And after testing and optimization, you'll find better methods of monetizing your own traffic.

When done properly, content marketing attracts prospects at the top of the funnel and guides them through the buyer journey until they convert to become customers. These are *conversions you would never have reached otherwise.*

And this is why it is important to give your content marketing program the time it takes to achieve the trust required for new prospects to convert.

Content marketing conversions are the prospects who became customers because of helpful, useful, and/or entertaining content your brand provided them.

EXAMPLE: HOW NOT TO DRIVE CONVERSIONS

While at SAP, Michael spent a year "getting conversion wrong." Following the pressure from product marketers and sales people, the first iteration of his content marketing site had dozens of links to product pages and opportunities for readers to click-to-call, click–to-chat, and email a sales representative.

After 12 months, thousands of articles published and a few hundred thousand visitors, the site had seen only a few dozen clicks on any of those "conversions." No one was reading their early-stage articles, and then looking for product information.

What they did find, however, was that visitors who subscribed to the site, were 10x more likely to convert. So they started focusing on conversions and more appropriate "middle-stage" offers like Ultimate Guides and events.

By the end of year two, the site had more than a thousand leads, event registrations and offer form completions.

The core metrics used to measure the business case are:

• Cost per lead
• Percentage of leads sourced
• Conversions

How to Calculate the Value of Cost per Lead

The cost per lead is the amount your brand spends to acquire a lead. Calculating content marketing's cost per lead is crucial in order to benchmark your program's effectiveness against other marketing programs. Determining this is simple. To begin, we need to know the costs accrued to create and distribute the content.

For this example, Software Inc. created two pieces of content. For the ROI Guide, the team spent **$3,000 to create and invested $10,000 to distribute.** For the Strategy Guide, the team also spent **$3,000 to create, but spent $20,000 to distribute.** Combining these costs, we can see that the ROI Guide cost **Software Inc. $13,000 and the Strategy Guide cost $23,000.**

Now that we know how much the content cost to create and distribute, let's see how the content performed in terms of lead generation to calculate cost per qualified lead.

Software Inc.'s ROI Guide generated **550 new leads, 205 of which were qualified leads.** To calculate cost per lead, we want to take the total cost ($13,000) divided by the total number of qualified leads (205).

PRICE OF ROI GUIDE PER QUALIFIED LEAD

$13,000 / 205 = $63

Therefore, the ROI Guide cost $63 per qualified lead.
To find the cost of the Strategy Guide, we will also take the total cost ($23,000) divided by the total number of qualified leads (130). **Therefore, the Strategy Guide cost $177 per qualified lead.**

VALUE
OF SOFTWARE

$23,000 / 130 = $177

To determine an accurate average total cost per lead of content marketing, we'd want to take a larger sample, but for the purpose of this book, we'll simplify and average these two costs.

AVERAGE TOTAL
COST PER LEAD

($63 + $177) / 2 = $120

Therefore, Software Inc.'s average total cost per lead for content marketing is $120.

How to Calculate the Value of Percentage of Leads Sourced

In order to determine the percentage of leads from Software Inc.'s content marketing, we first need to gather the total number of leads sourced from other marketing programs.

Looking at the data gathered in Graphic G, we see that Software

Inc.'s content marketing accounts for 205 of its total 710 marketing qualified leads.

To find the percentage, we divide the total number of leads sourced (710) divided by the number of leads sourced from the content program (205). **Therefore, we can determine that Software Inc.'s content marketing accounts for 28.9% of total qualified leads.**

Depending on the goals and expectations from your marketing leadership, you can gauge how well your content is performing compared to other marketing programs.

GRAPHIC G

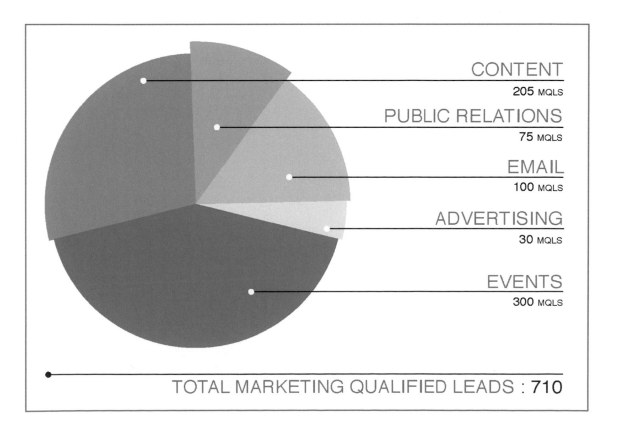

CONTENT
205 MQLS

PUBLIC RELATIONS
75 MQLS

EMAIL
100 MQLS

ADVERTISING
30 MQLS

EVENTS
300 MQLS

TOTAL MARKETING QUALIFIED LEADS : 710

How to Calculate the Value of Conversion

Conversions are the percentage of people who take a desired action. To determine the **actual revenue sourced by content marketing**, we need to look at conversions.

For this example, Software Inc.'s content marketing has a conversion rate of 50% and the average sale is worth $500. To find the total conversions, we need to multiply our total qualified leads by 50%.

VALUE OF
CONVERSION

205 X 50% = 102.5 conversion

Based on that finding, we assume these sales will average $500, so **to find the total value we multiply the conversions (102.5) by the average sale ($500).**

TOTAL
CONVERSIONS

102.5 X $500 = $51,000

Therefore, Software Inc.'s **total content marketing conversions are worth $51,000.**

Again, in order to gauge the performance of this conversion value, Software Inc. will want to do some discovery within their organization to see how it stacks up against other marketing departments. (For more information on this, please reference Part One.)

As we've seen time and time again, the companies that commit to measuring the value of leads or sales generated from content marketing, when compared to the value of leads or sales generated from other marketing programs, are able to demonstrate significant return on their content marketing programs.

Retention

Retention is sometimes left out of the marketing measurement discussion, but the value of one retained customer has been shown to be much more profitable than new customers[15]. Consider:

• The Lifetime Value of one retained customers is as much as five times the Lifetime Value of a new customer.
• Repeat customers spend one-third more than new ones.
• A 5% increase in retention increases the ROI of marketing by 25% to 95%.
• A 10% increase in retention yields a 30% rise in the value of the company.

Many of our customers have shown the vision to focus on providing value to existing customers through content marketing. But what is the return on that investment and how can you measure it?

How to Calculate the Value of Retention

It starts by developing your content marketing program tied to the same website where your existing customers login or where you can track interaction with content and purchases made on your ecommerce site.

Your customers' information needs don't stop once they start paying you. So plan, deliver and optimize content for your repeat visitors and existing customers.

Once you've started delivering content for customers, you can track the retention rate and the spend rate for customers who interact with content and compare that to customers who have not.

Based on that segmentation, you can track the value of your content marketing for existing customers based on both retention rate and spend levels.

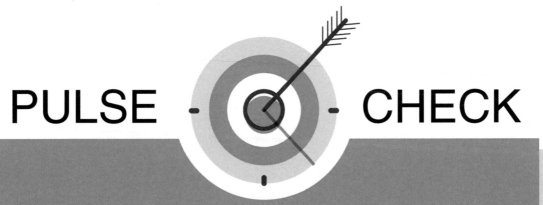

PULSE - ⦿ - CHECK

CONVERSIONS AND RETENTION

1. To show the cost savings of content marketing, measure the cost per lead of content marketing vs. average marketing cost per lead

2. To measure the value of content marketing leads, calculate the percentage of leads from content marketing and multiply by the average marketing cost per lead

3. Or, calculate the number of leads from content marketing and multiply by the average cost per lead

4. To track the value of content marketing on retention, track retention rates and total spend for customers who engage with your content marketing and compare that with customers who have not engaged with your content marketing.

<u>NOTES</u>

YOUR CONTENT FORMULA
CHEAT SHEETS

So what's MY Content Marketing ROI?

If you think this book was TL/DR (Too Long / Didn't Read) here's an action plan in 10 steps and with 10 calculations to help you identify your own Content Formula.

10 Steps
to develop your Content Formula

 1. Google "what is [your product category]?" **If your company's website doesn't show up in the top three search results, you are missing an opportunity to reach, engage and convert potential customers at the beginning of their buying journey.**

 2. Does your brand achieve a fair "share of voice" **in online conversations about your product category relative to your market share and that of your competition?**

 3. Take a sample of the content your business creates and identify the cost, usage and performance of that content. **Chances are you will find more than fifty percent never gets used at all (pure waste.) Shift that wasted content production into a content marketing program.**

 4. What percent of the traffic on your website comes from early-stage search? **What percent of the content on your website answers early-stage customer questions.**

 5. How much quantifiable brand engagement (traffic to your website) does your traditional marketing generate? **Shift some of that budget to content marketing so you can track your results.**

6. What have you spent on paid search because you don't rank for key search terms organically? **Every organic visitor can be seen as money saved.**

 7. How big is your content subscriber list? **Every subscriber to your content marketing program provides reach, engagement and the potential to convert to real sales.**

 8. What is the cost per lead **of your content marketing program vs. traditional outbound approaches like direct response, cold calling, email list rentals and banners ads?**

 9. What percentage of your marketing-generated revenue comes from content marketing?

 10. What is the lifetime value and retention rate **of your customers who engage with your content marketing vs. those who don't?**

If you can answer these 10 questions, you have all the information you need to develop your own Content Formula!

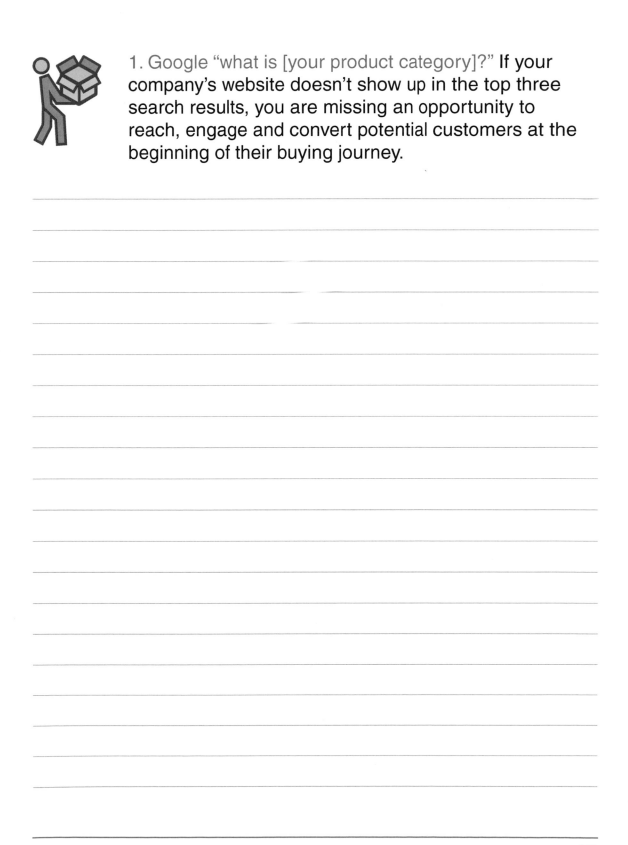

1. Google "what is [your product category]?" If your company's website doesn't show up in the top three search results, you are missing an opportunity to reach, engage and convert potential customers at the beginning of their buying journey.

2. Does your brand achieve a fair "share of voice" in online conversations about your product category relative to your market share and that of your competition?

 3. Take a sample of the content your business creates and identify the cost, usage and performance of that content. Chances are you will find more than 50% never gets used at all (pure waste.) Shift that wasted content production into a content marketing program.

4. What percent of the traffic on your website comes from early-stage search? **What percent of the content on your website answers early-stage customer questions.**

5. How much quantifiable brand engagement (traffic to your website) does your traditional marketing generate? Shift some of that budget to content marketing so you can track your results.

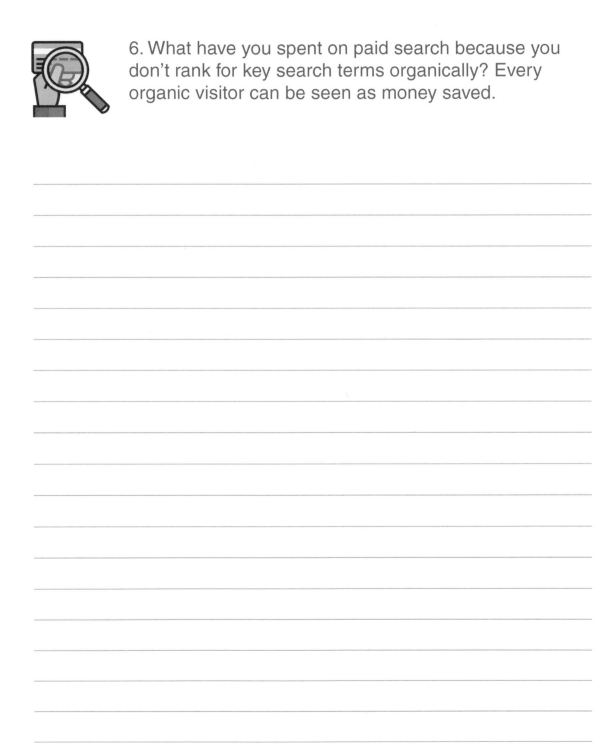

6. What have you spent on paid search because you don't rank for key search terms organically? Every organic visitor can be seen as money saved.

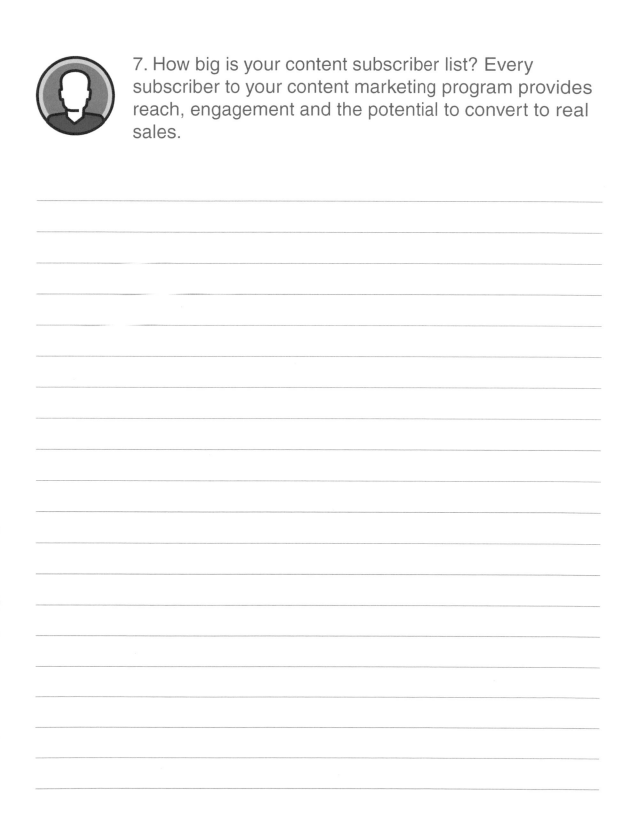

7. How big is your content subscriber list? Every subscriber to your content marketing program provides reach, engagement and the potential to convert to real sales.

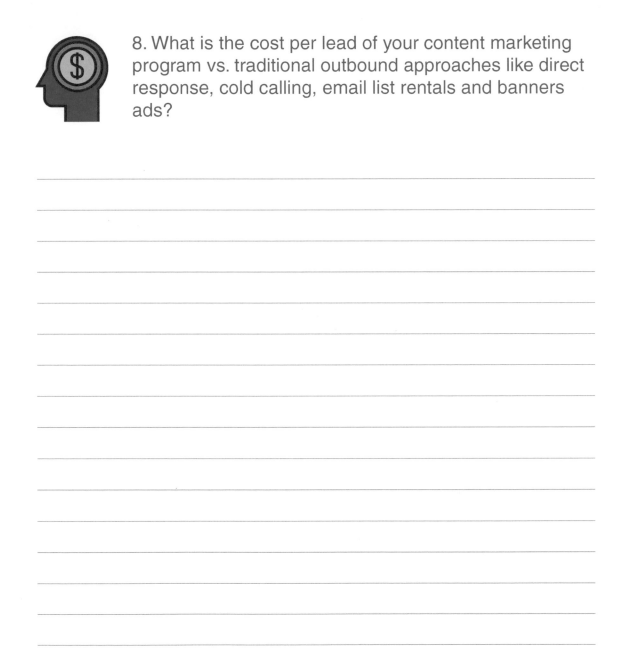

8. What is the cost per lead of your content marketing program vs. traditional outbound approaches like direct response, cold calling, email list rentals and banners ads?

9. What percentage of your marketing-generated revenue comes from content marketing?

10. What is the lifetime value and retention rate of your customers who engage with your content marketing vs. those who don't?

10 Calculations
to develop your **Content Formula**

Here is a quick cheat sheet for you to calculate your own content marketing ROI:

1. How Much Money Are You Wasting on Unused Content?
   Current costs
   * Amount that gets used

2. What is the Value of Organic Search?
   (Budget for Paid Search
   * Organic Search Traffic)
   / Paid Search Traffic

3. What is the Value of Unbranded Organic Search Traffic?
   (Paid Search Budget * Organic Search Traffic)
   / Paid Search Traffic

4. What is Your Fair Share of Voice Index?
   (Online share of organic search Traffic
   / Market Share)
   * 100

5. What is the Value of Our Repeat Visitors?
   (Website Advertising Dollars /Ad-driven Traffic) *
   Repeat Visitors

6. What is the Value of a Subscriber?
    (# of Subscribers * Avg. Sale Price
    * (1 – Unsubscribe Rate) – # of Subscribers
    * Cost per Acquisition) / # of Subscribers)

7. What is the Value of a Subscriber?
    (If you know sales generated from email nurture)
    Sales Generated From Email
    / # of Subscribers

8. What is the Content Marketing Cost
    Per Lead?
    Content Marketing Costs
    / Content Marketing Leads

9. What is the Value of Content Marketing Leads?
    Content Marketing Leads * Content Marketing
    Conversion Rate * Avg. Sale Price
    [OR]
    % of Leads from Content Marketing Costs * Avg.
    Lead Conversion Rate * Avg. Sale Price

10. What is the Value of Content Marketing Retention?
    Spend From Customers Who Don't Engage in
    Content – Spend From Customer Who Do Engage in
    Your Content

 1. How Much Money Are You Wasting on
Unused Content?
Current costs * Amount that gets used

2.What is the Value of Organic Search?
**(Budget for Paid Search * Organic Search Traffic)
/ Paid Search Traffic**

 3. What is the Value of Unbranded Organic Search Traffic?
(Paid Search Budget * Organic Search Traffic) / Paid Search Traffic

4. What is Your Fair Share of Voice Index?
(Online share of organic search Traffic / Market Share) * 100

5. What is the Value of Our Repeat Visitors?
(Website Advertising Dollars /Ad-driven Traffic)
* Repeat Visitors

6. What is the Value of a Subscriber?
(# of Subscribers * Avg. Sale Price *
 (1 – Unsubscribe Rate) – # of Subscribers
* Cost per Acquisition) / # of Subscribers)

7. What is the Value of a Subscriber? (If you know sales generated from email nurture)

Sales Generated From Email / # of Subscribers

8. What is the Content Marketing Cost Per Lead?
Content Marketing Costs / Content Marketing Leads

9. What is the Value of Content Marketing Leads?
Content Marketing Leads * Content Marketing
Conversion Rate * Avg. Sale Price
[OR]
% of Leads from Content Marketing Costs * Avg. Lead
Conversion Rate * Avg. Sale Price

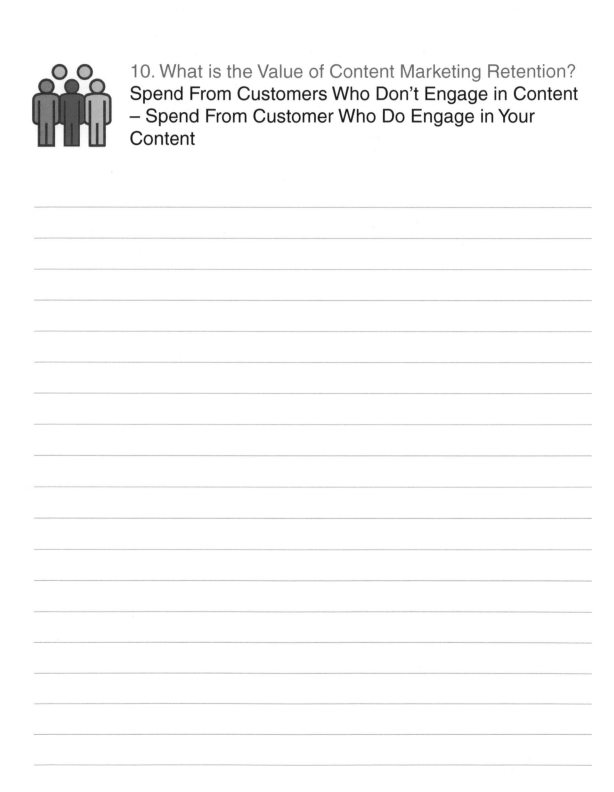

10. What is the Value of Content Marketing Retention?
Spend From Customers Who Don't Engage in Content – Spend From Customer Who Do Engage in Your Content